Professor Pete's Prehistoric Animals

ARMOURED DINOSAURS

W

FRANKLIN WATTS

LONDON·SYDNEY

Franklin Watts
This edition published in the UK in 2017 by The Watts Publishing Group

Designed and illustrated by David West

ISBN 978 1 4451 5500 5

Printed in Malaysia

Franklin Watts
An imprint of
Hachette Children's Group
Part of The Watts Publishing Group
Carmelite House
50 Victoria Embankment
London EC4Y 0DZ

An Hachette UK Company.
www.hachette.co.uk

www.franklinwatts.co.uk

PROFESSOR PETE'S PREHISTORIC ANIMALS ARMOURED DINOSAURS
was produced for Franklin Watts by
David West Children's Books, 6 Princeton Court, 55 Felsham Road, London SW15 1AZ

Professor Pete says:
This little guy will tell you something more about the animal.

Learn what this animal ate.

Where and when (Mya=Millions of Years Ago) did it live?

Its size is revealed!

How fast or slow was it?

Discover the meaning of its name.

A timeline on page 24 shows you the dates of the different periods in Mya.

Contents

Ampelosaurus

am-pel-oh-sore-us

This long-necked dinosaur is a **sauropod**, unlike most of the dinosaurs in this book.

The one thing it does have in common with them is its spiky armoured skin. **Predators** such as a Tyrannosaurus would have found it difficult to chew its way through the armour.

Ampelosaurus was a plant eater

 Ampelosaurus means 'vineyard lizard'.

 It lived in France during the Upper Cretaceous period, 71–65 Mya.

 Ampelosaurus grew up to 15 metres in length and weighed 9 tonnes.

 It might have been able to reach a speed of 24 kilometres per hour.

Professor Pete says:
Ampelosaurus was a member of the giant, long-necked dinosaurs known as titanosaurs.

5

Ankylosaurus was a plant eater.

 The top speed of Ankylosaurus was only 9 kilometres per hour.

 Ankylosaurus grew up to 7 metres long and weighed 5.3 tonnes.

 It lived in Canada and the United States during the Upper Cretaceous period, 74–67 Mya.

 Ankylosaurus means 'fused lizard', after the oval bony nodules 'fused' into its skin.

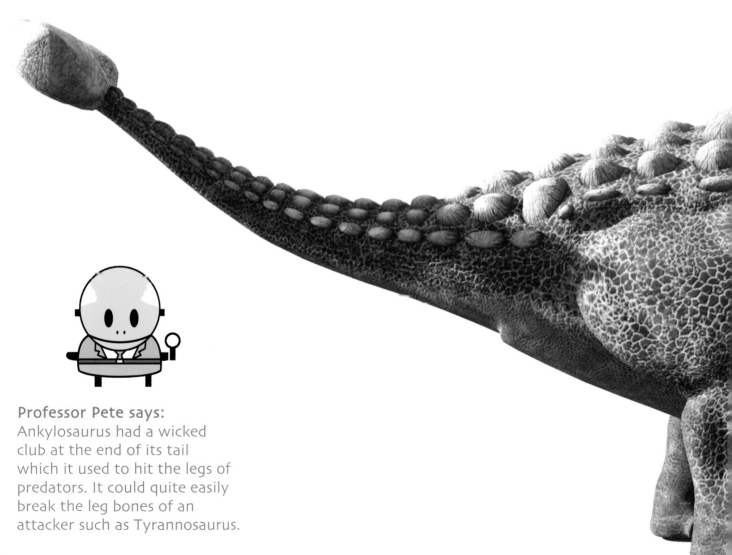

Professor Pete says:
Ankylosaurus had a wicked club at the end of its tail which it used to hit the legs of predators. It could quite easily break the leg bones of an attacker such as Tyrannosaurus.

Ankylosaurus

an-KIE-loh-sore-us

Ankylosaurus was protected from predators by thick, leathery skin from which bony, oval nodules grew, called osteoderms.

Desmatosuchus was a plant eater. It probably ate low-lying vegetation.

Desmatosuchus was heavily armoured and not very fast.

Desmatosuchus grew up to 5 metres in length and weighed 226.7–453.6 kilogrammes.

It lived in the United States during the Upper Triassic period, 230 Mya.

Desmatosuchus means 'link crocodile'.

8

Desmatosuchus

dez-MAT-oh-SOO-kuss

Although not a dinosaur this armoured beast was a relative of the dinosaurs. It was hunted by early meat-eating dinosaurs. As well as armour, it had enormous spikes growing outwards from its shoulders and neck.

Professor Pete says:
Desmatosuchus had a pig-like snout which gave it a comical appearance.

It lived in Canada and the United States during the Upper Cretaceous period, 76–70 Mya.

Euoplocephalus was probably a slow-moving dinosaur, travelling no faster than 9 kilometres per hour.

Euoplocephalus grew up to 7 metres in length and weighed 3.6 tonnes.

Euoplocephalus means 'well-armoured head'.

Euoplocephalus was a plant eater.

Professor Pete says:
With the discovery of more than 40 almost complete skeletons, Euoplocephalus is the best-known ankylosaur among **paleontologists**.

Euoplocephalus

you-oh-plo-kef-ah-luss

Euoplocephalus was very similar to Ankylosaurus. It had a tail club and thick, leathery skin covered in bony nodules, some of which formed spikes. Even its eyelids were armoured.

Hungarosaurus was a plant eater. It probably ate low-lying vegetation.

Hungarosaurus was heavily armoured and unlikely to have run faster than 16 kilometres per hour.

Hungarosaurus grew up to 4 metres in length and weighed 500 kilogrammes.

It lived in Hungary during the Upper Cretaceous period, 98–65 Mya.

Hungarosaurus means 'Hungarian lizard'.

Hungarosaurus

hun-ger-oh-SORE-us

Hungarosaurus had excellent armour along the top of its body. It had two rows of sharp spikes growing from its neck to halfway down its tail. It had no tail club though.

Professor Pete says:
Hungarosaurus had a strange shape. Its front legs were longer than its back legs.

Kaprosuchus

CAP-roh-SOO-kuss

This ferocious, armoured beast was not a dinosaur but a type of **crocodilian** that lived on land. It roamed the plains of Africa hunting plant-eating dinosaurs.

Kaprosuchus grew up to 6.1 metres in length and weighed around 454–907 kilogrammes.

Kaprosuchus was quite agile and could probably move quite fast.

It lived in Niger, Africa during the Lower Cretaceous period, 100–95 Mya.

Kaprosuchus was a meat eater.

Kaprosuchus means 'boar crocodile'.

Professor Pete says:
This scary beast had strange horns sticking out from behind its eyes and three sets of tusk-like teeth.

Pachycephalosaurus grew up to 4.6 metres in length and weighed about 454 kilogrammes.

 Pachycephalosaurus moved on two legs but was probably not a fast runner.

 It lived in the United States during the Upper Cretaceous period, 75–65 Mya.

 Pachycephalosaurus was a plant eater.

 Pachycephalosaurus means 'thick-headed lizard'.

16

Pachycephalosaurus

pack-i-KEF-al-oh-sore-russ

This dinosaur had a heavily armoured head that was not only for protection. It was used to butt opponents during the mating season, like deer do today.

Professor Pete says:
Paleontologists think their heads might have been used in self defence. Their hard skulls and spiky edges could have caused serious injuries to their attackers.

Polacanthus

pol-ah-KAN-thus

Polacanthus had a great armoury
of spikes and armour plate.
It did not have a
tail club.

Professor Pete says:
If attacked by a predator,
Polacanthus used its tail as a
defensive weapon. As it whipped
its tail sideways the spikes on the
edges acted like hedge cutters!

Polacanthus was a plant eater and fed on a variety of plants.

Polacanthus means 'many spikes'.

It lived in England during the Lower Cretaceous period, 125 Mya.

Polacanthus was a slow-moving dinosaur that could probably reach 9 kilometres per hour.

Polacanthus grew up to 5 metres long and weighed 1.8 tonnes.

19

Sauropelta

sore-oh-pelt-ah

This armoured dinosaur had large spikes growing from its neck and shoulders. Its back was armoured with thick, leathery skin studded with bony nodules.

Professor Pete says:
If attacked by predators Sauropelta would lie down to protect its unarmoured underside.

Sauropelta ate plants.

 Sauropelta means 'lizard shield'.

 Sauropelta was 4.6 metres long and weighed around 0.9–1.8 tonnes.

 Sauropelta could twist and turn but was not able to run very fast.

 It lived in the United States during the Lower Cretaceous period, 120–110 Mya.

Talarurus

tal-ah-ROOR-us

Although similar to an Ankylosaurus this armoured plant eater was slightly smaller. It had bony nodules embedded in thick, leathery skin, and a wicked clubbed tail.

Professor Pete says:
Its armoured tail, held rigid by stiff tendons, had a club of fused bones at its end. Strong muscles at the base of the tail allowed it to be swung with great force at an attacker such as Tarbosaurus.

Talarurus may not have been able to run fast, but it could spin quickly to hit its attacker with its tail!

 Talarurus lived in Mongolia during the Upper Cretaceous period, 98–88 Mya.

 Talarurus means 'wicker tail' from the wicker-like tendons that stiffened its tail.

 Talarurus ate plants.

 It measured up to 6 metres long and weighed up to 0.9 tonnes.

Glossary

crocodilian
Of a group of animals that includes crocodiles.

paleontologists
Scientists who study early forms of life.

predators
Animals that hunt and eat other animals.

sauropod
Huge plant-eating dinosaur with a long neck and tail, a small head and massive limbs with five toes.

wicker
Pliable twigs woven to make items such as furniture and baskets.

Timeline

Dinosaurs lived during the Mesozoic Era which is divided into three main periods.

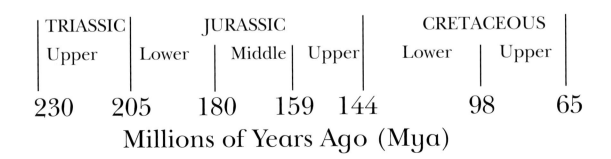

TRIASSIC		JURASSIC			CRETACEOUS	
Upper	Lower	Middle	Upper		Lower	Upper
230	205	180	159	144	98	65

Millions of Years Ago (Mya)